# All About Sunlight

Charmaine Robertson

Rosen REAL READERS

Rosen Classroom™
New York

I0809768

Sunlight comes from the sun.
The sun is a star.

The sun gives off heat and light.

The sun is very strong.

It is important to wear sunblock.

Sunlight gives Earth energy.

Plants need sunlight to grow.

People and animals eat plants.

People need sunlight! Sunlight helps people stay healthy.

# Words to Know

animal

Earth

plant

sun